# WE ♥ BILLIE EILISH

## HER LIFE    HER MUSIC    HER STORY

MW01129986

MORTIMER

Published in 2020 by Mortimer Children's Books
An Imprint of Welbeck Children's Limited, part of Welbeck
Publishing Group.

20 Mortimer Street London W1T 3JW

Text & design © 2020 Welbeck Children's Limited,
part of Welbeck Publishing Group.

Designed, written and packaged by: Dynamo Limited
Art editor: Deborah Vickers
Editor: Jenni Lazell
Picture research: Paul Langan

All rights reserved. No part of this publication may be reproduced, stored in a
retrieval system, or transmitted in any form or by any means, electronically,
mechanical, photocopying, recording, or otherwise, without the prior permission
of the copyright owners and the publishers.

ISBN 978-1-83935-032-0

Printed in Dubai
10 9 8 7 6 5 4 3 2

The publishers would like to thank the following sources for
their kind permission to reproduce the pictures in this book.
Key: T=top, B=bottom, L=left, R=right, C=center.

GETTY IMAGES: /Mireya Acierto: 60BR; /Craig Barritt: 14T; /
Robyn Beck/AFP: 79; /Leon Bennett/WireImage: 41T, 66; /Paul
Bergen/Redferns: 67; /Monty Brinton/CBS: 56-57; /Frederic J
Brown/AFP: 30; /Frederick M Brown: 38BR; /Gareth Cattermole:
39BR; /Mary Clavering/Young Hollywood: 21, 60TR; /Lester
Cohen: 60BL; /Gregg DeGuire/FilmMagic: 19; /FilmMagic: 53T; /
Rich Fury: 15T, 22BR, 34-35, 39TL, 50-51, 73, 80; /Noam Galai:
61TL; /Frazer Harrison: 23TR, 48R; /Mat Hayward: 2; /Taylor
Hill: 10-11, 71L; /Nicholas Hunt/WireImage: 13, 38BL; /Samir
Hussein/WireImage: 45, 71TL; /Simone Joyner: 77; /Rick Kern/
WireImage: 53B; /Rob Kim: 41CT, 54, 60TL; /Roger Kisby: 46B; /
Jon Kopaloff/FilmMagic: 52, 61BL; /Jeff Kravitz/FilmMagic:
18BL; /Jean-Baptiste Lacroix/AFP: 61BR; /Scott Legato: 22TR,
71R; /Morgan Lieberman/FilmMagic: 39TR; /Kevin Mazur: 8,
22BL, 71BR; /Emma McIntyre: 29; /Sarah Morris/FilmMagic:
44R; /Tim Mosenfelder: 24-25, 27; /Katja Ogrin/Redferns: 49BR;
/Okea: 9L; /JC Olivera: 46T; /Terence Patrick/CBS: 33B, 71B; /
Marc Piasecki/GC Images: 23L, 61TR; /Rich Polk: 32T; /
Francesco Prandoni/Redferns: 15B; /Alberto E Rodriguez: 47B; /
Steve Russell/Toronto Star: 72T; /Rebecca Sapp/WireImage:
32B; /Donato Sardella: 55; /Amy Sussman: 18R, 39BL, 78; /
Denise Truscello: 6; /Kevin Winter: 7, 14-15, 48BL, 71TR; /David
Wolff Patrick/Redferns: 74-75
SHUTTERSTOCK: 9R; /Action Press: 72B; /Evan Agostini/
Invision/AP: 59; /Koury Angelo/Rolling Stone: 68-69; /Christian
Bertrand: 42-43; /Diane Bondareff/Invision/AP: 47T; /
Broadimage: 31; /David Buchan: 38TR; /Amy Harris/Invision/
AP: 64-65; /Ben Houdijk: 16-17, 37; /IBL: 5; /Invision/AP: 23BR;
/Rob Latour: 70; /Chelsea Lauren/Variety: 49T; /John Locher/
AP: 1; /Stephen Lovekin: 4; /MediaPunch: 12, 63; /Gregory Pace:
41B; /Christopher Polk: 36, 44BL; /Geoff Pugh: 41CB; /Sara
Jaye Weiss: 33T

# CONTENTS

# WELCOME

Welcome to your one-stop guide to all things Billie Eilish—the future of pop. Whether you're a superfan, a total newbie, or somewhere in between, this book is packed with everything you need to know about this global icon.

How did Billie go from making music in her bedroom to being the most talked about teen on the planet? Being 100 percent Billie, that's how! She has buckets of talent, and people can't get enough of her attitude. Billie is unapologetic about who she is. Being authentic is what people love most about her.

## LEAD, DON'T FOLLOW

Billie isn't a fan of rules. She's breaking the polished pop-star mold and making being grungy the new cool. She loves her oversized clothes, and she isn't afraid to take artistic risks. Billie proves that you don't have to behave like other pop stars to make it big.

Being all kinds of brave means that Billie isn't afraid to share her vision through song-writing and directing music videos. Plus, her "homemade" tunes totally rule the charts, proving that you don't always need a fancy recording studio to make a hit. So, who's ready to join Billie's Pirates? (That's what she calls her fans, FYI.)

# PHENOMENON

It was 2015 when Billie went from an unknown 14-year-old to one of the world's most watched and most loved musical phenomena.

## FUSION

Billie's sound is a blend of different musical genres – EDM, jazz, electro-pop, and hip-hop fused together to make one totally unique sound. Inspired by her life experiences and vivid dreams, each song has its own unique vibe.

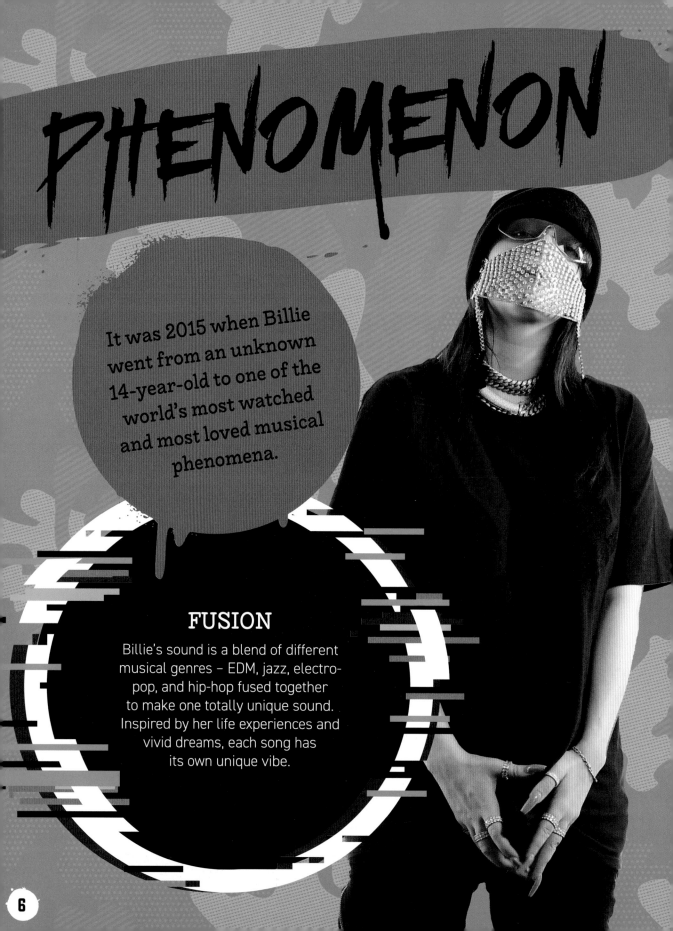

## VOICE OF A GENERATION

With over 40 million followers on social media, Billie uses her influence for good by speaking for an entire generation. Just like climate change activist Greta Thunberg, she is focused on ensuring young people are heard. "Teenagers know more about the country that we're living in right now than anybody," she says. ". . . To see young people taking part in peaceful protests, and not obeying, is beautiful."

## TAKING THE CROWN

Fast-forward to 2020, when Billie made history by winning five Grammy Awards. She became the youngest person ever to win Best Album, taking the crown from Taylor Swift. Turn to page 44 for more awards!

# MEET BILLIE

She's the most talked about teen on the planet, but how much do we really know about the megastar that is Billie Eilish?

BROTHER—FINNEAS

MOM—MAGGIE

DAD—PATRICK

BILLIE

Billie started writing music when she was 11 years old. She grew up in Los Angeles in a family of musicians and actors.

**FULL NAME:** Billie Eilish Pirate Baird O'Connell

**DATE OF BIRTH:** December 18, 2001

**HEIGHT:** 5 ft. 4 in. (1.61m)

**STAR SIGN:** Sagittarius

## HOBBIES:

- Acting
- Dancing—Billie took lessons growing up
- Moviemaking—she liked to film and edit shorts
- Singing—Billie was part of the Los Angeles Children's Choir

## PETS:
Billie has a pet tarantula.

## FAVE TV SHOW:
*The Office* (U.S.)

## FAVE MUSIC

She's a Belieber, AKA a Justin Bieber fan. She also says The Beatles and Avril Lavigne were the soundtrack to her childhood.

### DID YOU KNOW?

Billie is vegan.

### DID YOU KNOW?

Billie was homeschooled.

## SIBLING GOALS:

Billie's brother is named Finneas. She cowrites her music with him, and he produces it. Find out more on page 18.

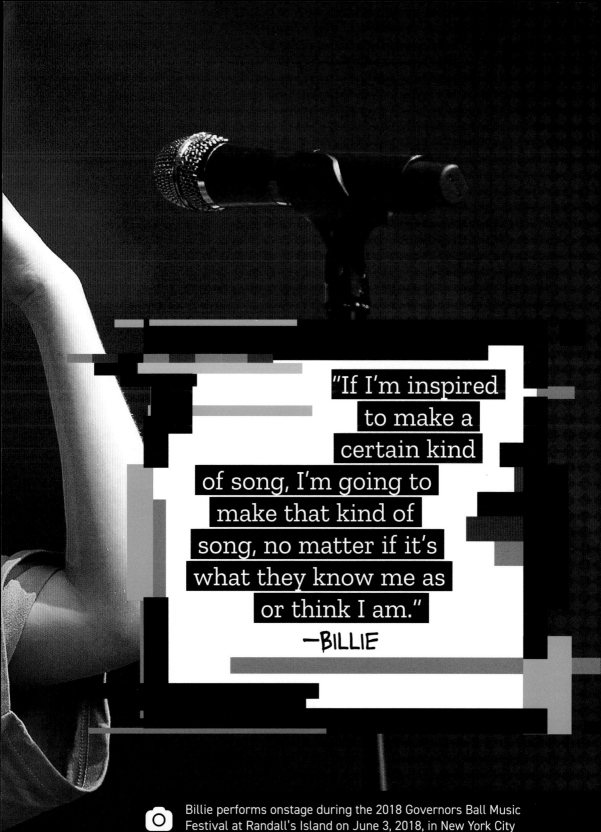

"If I'm inspired to make a certain kind of song, I'm going to make that kind of song, no matter if it's what they know me as or think I am."

—BILLIE

Billie performs onstage during the 2018 Governors Ball Music Festival at Randall's Island on June 3, 2018, in New York City

# THE STORY SO FAR...

Billie has managed to squeeze a lot into her life so far! Let's take a look at her time in the spotlight, from SoundCloud to world domination.

## GROWING UP

Billie and her brother, Finneas, lived with their parents, Maggie and Patrick, who were in the entertainment industry. It was a musical home with three pianos and plenty of ukuleles! She and Finneas spent their childhood writing songs in their bedrooms.

## FAME

At 14, Billie shot to fame after uploading "ocean eyes" to SoundCloud. The track, which was written by Finneas, grabbed the world's attention. "ocean eyes" was originally recorded for Billie's dance class. It was so great they decided to share it on SoundCloud, and the rest is music history.

## TAKING OFF

After the music video with Billie dancing to "ocean eyes" was released, record labels were quickly fighting to represent her. Interscope Records officially released the track to the world, followed by "six feet under" soon after. Billie went on to release her debut EP, *don't smile at me,* in August 2017, with the Where's My Mind? tour following in 2018.

## YOU SHOULD SEE ME ON TV

As you'd expect, Billie has popped up on plenty of TV shows. Her first daytime TV appearance was on *The Ellen DeGeneres Show.* She wowed the audience when she performed "you should see me in a crown." She joined James Corden on *Carpool Karaoke,* which made fans very happy! We got a sneak peek into the star's home, and she even introduced James to her pet spider.

## LOVING LIFE IN 2019

2019 was a big year for Billie. It started well when DJ Zane Lowe predicted that Eilish would be the star of the year, and of course he was right. It was the year Billie became a household name. From lighting up the festival scene at Coachella, Glastonbury, and Reading to featuring in a Calvin Klein campaign! Then the nominations and awards began rolling in. Turn to page 44 to find out more!

## MILLENNIUM HERO

Her first full-length album, *When We All Fall Asleep, Where Do We Go?*, was released in March 2019. It entered the Billboard 200 chart at number one. This made Billie a record breaker. Hers was the first number one album in the U.S. by someone born in the 2000s.

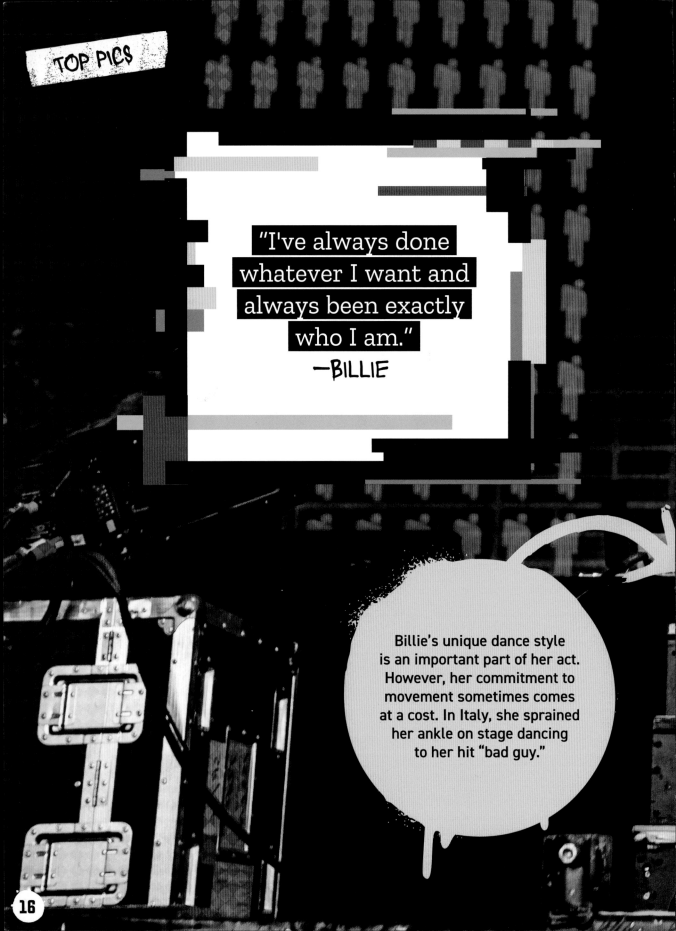

TOP PICS

"I've always done whatever I want and always been exactly who I am."
—BILLIE

Billie's unique dance style is an important part of her act. However, her commitment to movement sometimes comes at a cost. In Italy, she sprained her ankle on stage dancing to her hit "bad guy."

Billie performs at the Lowlands Festival in The Netherlands, August 2019

# MEET FINNEAS

A book about Billie wouldn't be complete without celebrating her mega-talented big brother, Finneas.

Don't go thinking Finneas is a silent sidekick. He's a super-successful actor, singer, songwriter, and record producer in his own right, too.

**DID YOU KNOW?**

He's in a band called The Slightlys.

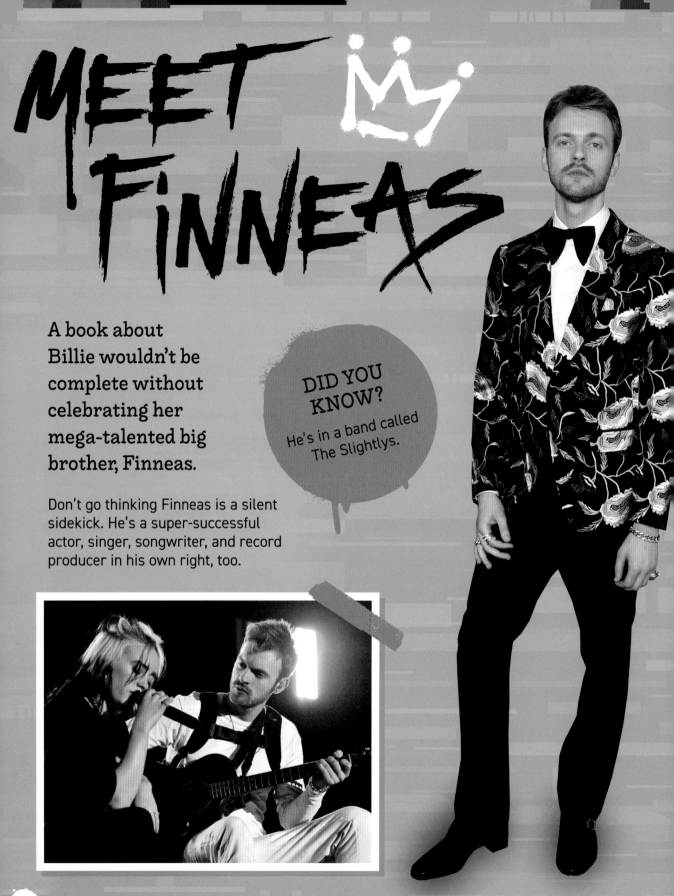

**FULL NAME:** Finneas Baird O'Connell

**DATE OF BIRTH:** July 30, 1997

**HEIGHT:** 6 ft. (182.9m)

**SIBLINGS:** Billie

**STAR SIGN:** Leo

## SOCIAL PLATFORMS:

**Instagram** over 2.1 million followers

**YouTube** over 630 thousand followers

**Twitter** over 280 thousand followers

As of March 2020

## GOING SOLO!

He's released his own songs, too.
Check out "Angel," "New Girl,"
and "I Lost a Friend."

## MOVIE CREDITS:

- *Bad Teacher* (2011)
- *Life Inside Out* (2013)

## TV APPEARANCES

He had a part in the hit TV series *Glee*. He played a character named Alistair. Finneas also played Ronnie Jr. in *Modern Family*!

"WE BOTH TAKE CRITICISM REALLY WELL. SO HE'LL DO SOMETHING AND I'LL BE LIKE, 'NO. THAT'S TERRIBLE,' AND HE'LL BE LIKE, 'OKAY. YOU'RE RIGHT.'"

—BILLIE ON FINNEAS

# DON'T SMILE  AT ME

This is the debut EP that catapulted Billie onto the global stage. Her songs blew critics and fans away! It was her moment, and she had everyone wanting to see and hear more.

## WHAT IS IT?

*don't smile at me* is Billie's debut EP (EP stands for extended play). It includes a lot of her previously released singles, including "ocean eyes," which has been streamed on Spotify over a billion times!

## TRACK LISTING:

### SIDE A
1. COPYCAT
2. indontwannabeyouanymore
3. my boy
4. watch

### SIDE B
5. party favor
6. bellyache
7. ocean eyes
8. hostage
9. &burn

## WHEN WAS IT RELEASED?

August 11, 2017–nine months after the release of "ocean eyes." Together, Billie and Finneas spent 18 months working on the EP.

## RE-RELEASE

In December 2017, Billie re-released the EP with a new track called "&burn." This was a collaboration with rapper Vince Staples.

Once the record dropped, it was impossible to ignore the Billie Eilish effect. Her growing fan base included big names such as Lorde and Julia Roberts. The world was well and truly watching, and they wanted more Billie.

## ON THE ROAD

Billie's whole family went on their first tour, just before *don't smile at me* was released. With a $100-a-night budget, it was far from glamorous! Her dad even quit his job to drive the tour van. Dedication!

# 10 REASONS WE LOVE

# BILLIE

There are way too many brilliant Billie things to squeeze onto one page, but we've given it a pretty good try!

**1**

Her family is her crew. They are tight and super-supportive of one another.

**2**

Billie cowrites all of her music—mainly with her brother.

**3** Being liked or cool isn't important. She's just true to herself!

**8**

Her hair colors are serious goals.

**4**

Billie loves customizing her fashion to make it one of a kind.

**5** She's all about being green and taking care of the environment. Check out her eco tour on page 36.

**6** People are already mimicking her style, and she was a popular Halloween costume choice in 2019.

**9**

Billie can play the piano, the guitar, and the ukulele.

**7** She speaks out about important issues that affect young people, such as mental health and body confidence.

**10** Billie represents total creative freedom. Her whole persona is experimental, exciting, and different. Awesome!

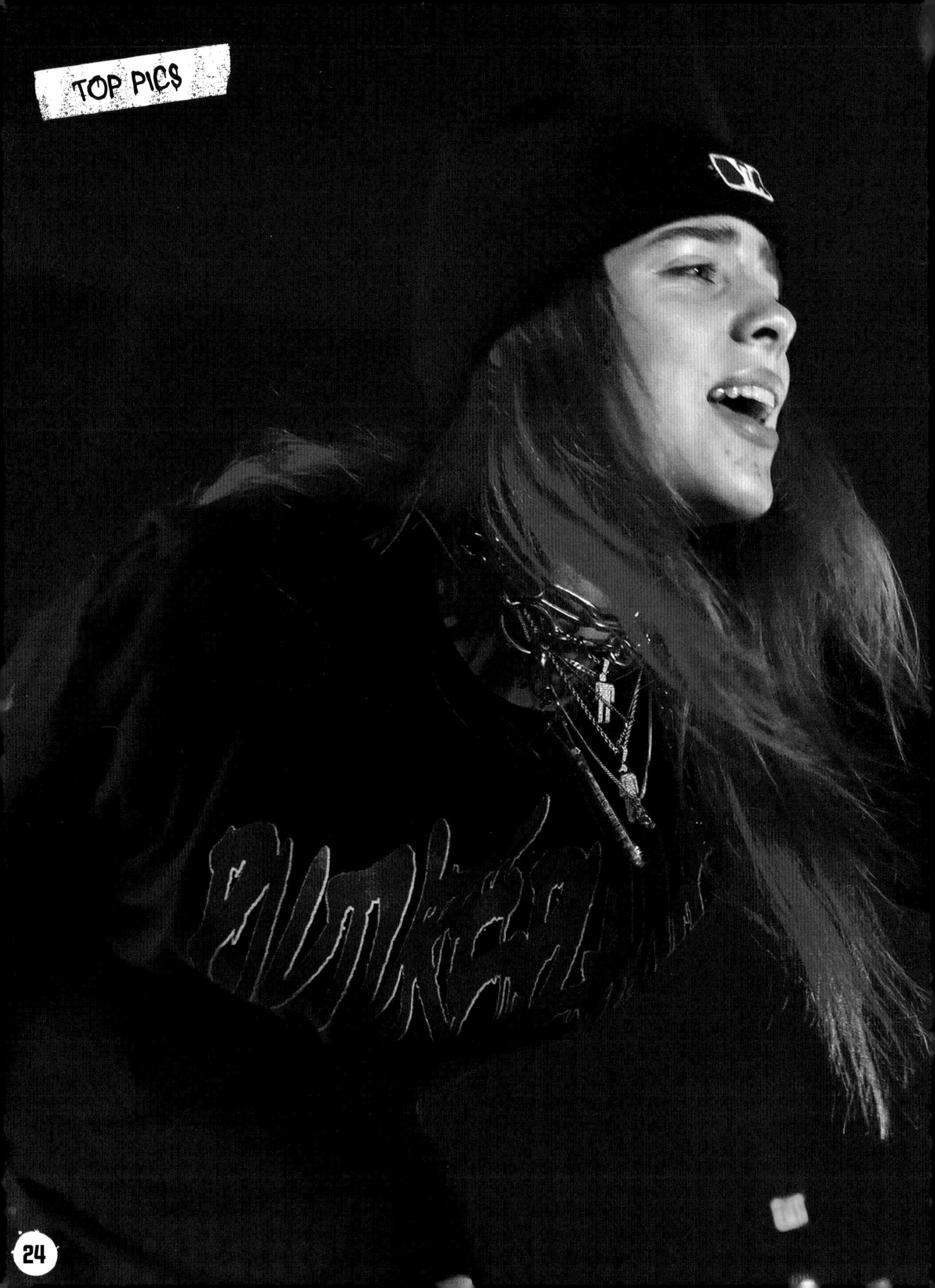

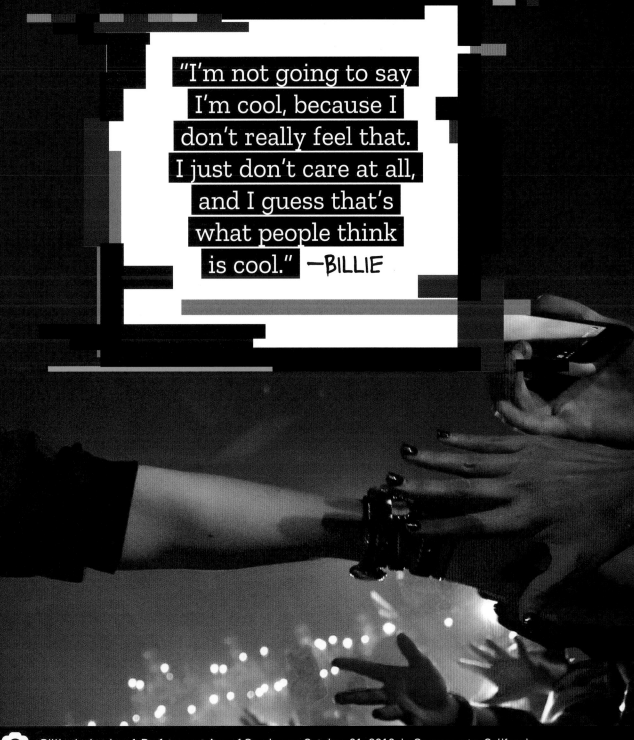

"I'm not going to say I'm cool, because I don't really feel that. I just don't care at all, and I guess that's what people think is cool." —BILLIE

Billie during her 1 By 1 tour at Ace of Spades on October 21, 2018, in Sacramento, California

# WHEN WE ALL FALL ASLEEP, WHERE DO WE GO?

After the huge success of *don't smile at me*, Billie didn't keep us waiting long before releasing new music into the world. She had proven that her unique style was just what the world was ready to hear!

## ALL CONQUERING

*When We All Fall Asleep, Where Do We Go?* could not have been received better. Critics and fans loved her first album with its dark and moody lyrics.

### TRACK LISTING:

1. !!!!!!!
2. bad guy
3. xanny
4. you should see me in a crown
5. all the good girls go to hell
6. wish you were gay
7. when the party's over
8. 8
9. my strange addiction
10. bury a friend
11. ilomilo
12. listen before i go
13. i love you
14. goodbye

EAR TO EAR

Guess what! Billie's music is created for when it is played into headphones. The music bounces from ear to ear for a perfect music experience.

## HOT 100

Billie's album broke a record for the most Top 100 songs by a woman! She had an impressive 14 tracks on the Billboard Top 100 at the same time.

## EVOLUTION

Comparing this album to her EP, it's clear that Billie's sound is evolving from whispering ballads like "ocean eyes." This album has more pop-hop, heavy beats, and synth sounds.

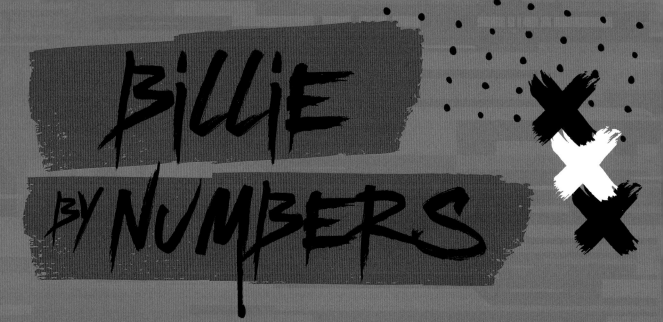

# BILLIE BY NUMBERS

**14** YEARS OLD WHEN **"OCEAN EYES"** was uploaded to SOUNDCLOUD

**1 BILLION** STREAMS BEFORE the release of her debut album

 *When We All Fall Asleep, Where Do We Go?* sold **313,000** units in its first week

OVER **25.1 MILLION** YOUTUBE SUBSCRIBERS JAN 2020

At 17, Billie was the youngest female soloist to top the UK album chart

**14** SONGS ON THE *BILLBOARD* TOP 100 IN 2019

OVER **2.3 BILLION** on-demand audio streams of her album *When We All Fall Asleep, Where Do We Go?* in 2019

**3** BILLIE PLAYS
MUSICAL
INSTRUMENTS
piano, guitar, and ukulele

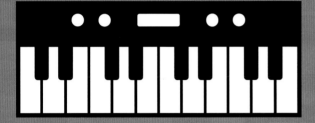

OVER
**49.6 MILLION**
INSTAGRAM FOLLOWERS
JAN 2020

OVER
**3.4 MILLION**
TWITTER
FOLLOWERS
JAN 2020

Billie won in all
the top 4 Grammy
categories in 2020

**6**

GRAMMY
NOMINATIONS
IN 2020

**1 BILLION**
STREAMS AT 17 YEARS OLD

# MUSIC VIDEOS

When an artist has millions of subscribers to her YouTube channel, they've got to be doing something right. Looking at Billie's music videos, it's clear to see why she has us all captivated.

## DIRECTOR

Billie prides herself on having creative control as an artist. Although some people didn't believe Billie had enough experience to direct a music video, she didn't give in! She has since directed some awesome videos, including "bored" and "six feet under."

## "XANNY"

### Directed by Billie

The first music video that Billie directed from her album *When We All Fall Asleep, Where Do We Go?* is minimalist, eerie, and powerful in its simplicity. It mainly involves Billie sitting on a bench, singing straight into the camera.

## "EVERYTHING I WANTED"

### Directed by Billie

This video begins with the words "Finneas is my brother and best friend. No matter what the circumstance, we have always and always will be there for each other" across the screen. It then shows them driving through the city together at night. They wrote the song together about each other.

## "BAD GUY"

This video starts with Billie kicking her way onto set and shows her riding around on a toy car! Expect lots of yellow, lots of high-energy dancing, and LOTS of attitude.

## "YOU SHOULD SEE ME IN A CROWN"

If you're not a creepy-crawly fan, then you may want to look away. However, if you're feeling brave, then this video is definitely worth checking out.

## "WHEN THE PARTY'S OVER"

This is the legendary music video where Eilish's eyes cry black, inky liquid. She's dressed in head-to-toe white and on an all-white set, making her electric blue hair and inky eyes really pop. You have to see it to believe it!

# SPEAK UP!

Billie is all about speaking out and smashing stereotypes. This teen is definitely not afraid to tell the world what she thinks, and she doesn't worry about fitting in!

## BREAK DOWN BARRIERS

Billie's message is that anything is possible! If you want to make music, you can do it from your home, and you don't need an expensive recording studio. Let's hope her story will inspire people from all backgrounds to follow their dreams.

Billie interviewed by KROQ Absolut Almost Acoustic Christmas in December 2018

## SHUT DOWN

Billie is the first to say something if her fans are nasty about another group or artist. When the media writes about rivalry between Billie and other stars, she shuts them down. If she spots her fans being mean to one another, she'll step in, too.

Billie speaks onstage at Spotlight, at the GRAMMY Museum, in September 2019

## FASHION REBEL

We all love Billie's iconic baggy clothes and oversized style. But there's a reason that she dresses like this! She doesn't want people to judge her based on her body shape.

Many female artists have spoken about industry pressure to look a certain way, so it's exciting to see Billie rebelling against what's expected! She's proven that being your true self is more important than fitting a certain image.

## SPEAK YOUR TRUTH

Billie was part of Calvin Klein's campaign I Speak My Truth in #MyCalvins. She doesn't want everybody to know everything about her, and why should they? The way we look and the clothes we wear is an individual choice.

Eilish debuted on *The Late Late Show with James Corden* in 2017 when she performed "ocean eyes."

Billie performs onstage during 102.7 KIIS FM's Jingle Ball on December 6, 2019, in Los Angeles, California

"There are always going to be bad things. But you can write it down and make a song out of it."
—BILLIE

# MAKE A CHANGE

Billie is outspoken, and she doesn't shy away from sharing her opinion. It's why we love her! Let's take a look at some of the matters that are close to Billie's heart.

## GREEN WORLD TOUR

Tackling climate change is a huge issue for many young people. No doubt fans were super excited to hear that it's a priority for Billie, too. In 2020, Billie planned to do her part with a green world tour, by collaborating with Reverb, a nonprofit arts organization that works with artists to find environmentally sustainable ways to do things. Plastic straws are banned, and fans must bring their own water bottles.

### FREE TICKETS!

By teaming up with the organization Global Citizens, Billie came up with a way for fans to earn free tickets to her tour. To earn them, all fans needed to do was take environmental action.

## ACTIVIST

Billie has been compared to the activist Greta Thunberg, but it's not just their youth they have in common. Like Greta, Billie is making it her mission to inspire a generation to speak out in defense of the environment. Both Greta and Billie believe in the power of their generation.

## POP RIVALRY

Billie doesn't want to be rivals with other pop stars. She likes to see other singers succeed. Did you see the moment she dedicated her 2020 Grammy award to Ariana Grande? Eilish has said how she doesn't want to be pitted against other female performers in the industry.

# STYLE ICON

Like most things Billie, when it comes to fashion, she makes her own rules! Which is your favorite look?

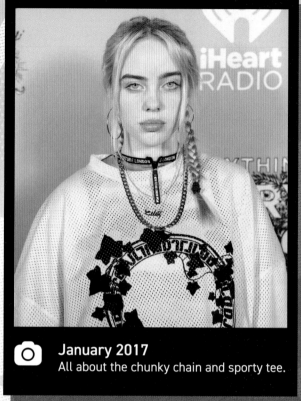

**January 2017**
All about the chunky chain and sporty tee.

**November 2017**
Bringing the bling in black and gold.

**April 2018**
Suddenly we want an orange anorak!

📷 **January 2019**
Black satin shirt? Why not!

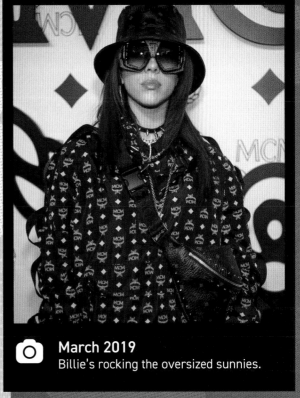

📷 **March 2019**
Billie's rocking the oversized sunnies.

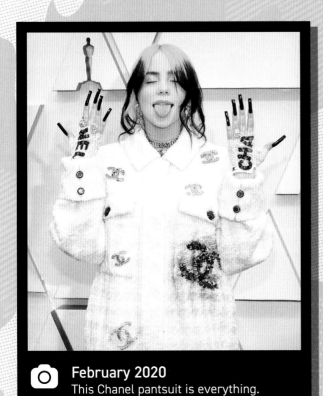

📷 **February 2020**
This Chanel pantsuit is everything.

📷 **February 2020**
Love her custom Burberry outfit teamed
with a PVC visor.

# WHAT IS YOUR BILLIE STYLE?

Try the quiz to reveal YOUR Billie look. Go on!

**START**

On weekends, you're most likely to be ...

In your room listening to music

Comedy or thriller?

Thriller

Comedy!

Is your style sporty?

Yep!

Fave Billie track?

"ocean eyes"

"bad guy"

Out and about with your friends!

Winter—I like wrapping up warm

Do you enjoy being center of attention?

Sometimes

Love it!

Summer or winter?

Summer because of all the colors!

What is your go-to accessory?

Earrings

**40**

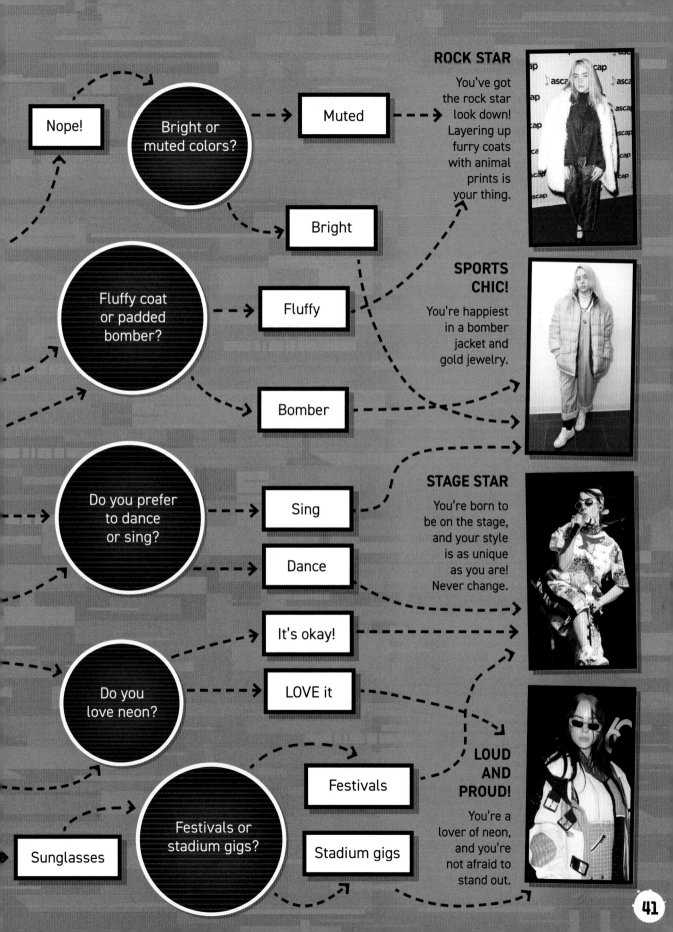

**ROCK STAR**

You've got the rock star look down! Layering up furry coats with animal prints is your thing.

**SPORTS CHIC!**

You're happiest in a bomber jacket and gold jewelry.

**STAGE STAR**

You're born to be on the stage, and your style is as unique as you are! Never change.

**LOUD AND PROUD!**

You're a lover of neon, and you're not afraid to stand out.

Nope!

Bright or muted colors?

Muted

Bright

Fluffy coat or padded bomber?

Fluffy

Bomber

Do you prefer to dance or sing?

Sing

Dance

It's okay!

Do you love neon?

LOVE it

Festivals

Sunglasses

Festivals or stadium gigs?

Stadium gigs

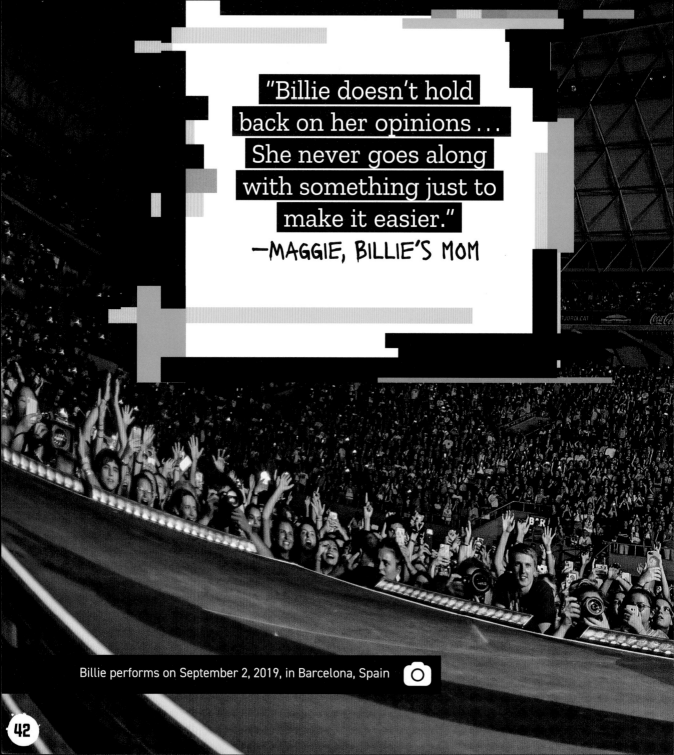

"Billie doesn't hold back on her opinions... She never goes along with something just to make it easier."

—MAGGIE, BILLIE'S MOM

Billie performs on September 2, 2019, in Barcelona, Spain

Eilish had the excitable crowd on their feet in Barcelona! Nobody can rock an orange two-piece better than she can!

# AWARD WINS

When it comes to winning big, Billie is your gal! With her record-breaking nominations and award wins, Billie is making history. Let's feast our eyes on her ever-growing trophy collection.

There's no denying that Billie is rewriting what it means to be a 21st-century pop star. In fact, she's thrown the rule book right out the window. The really exciting thing is that Billie is being recognized for all of this. She totally owned 2019, and we reckon it's going to continue for a long time.

**Ascap Vanguard Award** 2019

**American Music Awards** 2019

## BRIT WIN 2020

Billie won Best International Female Artist at the 2020 Brit Awards. It was also the first time that she performed "No Time to Die"—the Bond theme song! More about this on page 79.

## 2019 AMAs

She performed "all the good girls go to hell" at the 2019 American Music Awards. Plus, she won two awesome awards.

🏆 Favorite Alternative Rock Artist

🏆 New Artist of the Year

## CHOICE AWARDS

🏆 Nickelodeon Kids' Choice Award 2019 for Favorite Breakout Artist

🏆 Teen Choice Award Winner for Choice Breakout Artist 2019

🏆 E! People's Choice Award for Favorite Female 2019

## 2019 UK CHART RECORD

*When We All Fall Asleep, Where Do We Go?* burst onto the UK charts at number 1. This achievement got Billie into the Guinness World Records, as she became the youngest female solo act to top the UK album charts.

## MTV 2019 WINS

🏆 Best Editing for "bad guy"

🏆 Best New Artist

🏆 Push Artist of the Year

As well as all these big wins, Billie was also nominated for another 7 awards!

YouTube Diamond Award 2019

Clio
Awards
2019

## 2020 GRAMMY NOMINATION HISTORY

At 18 years old, Billie made Grammy Awards history. She was the youngest artist to be nominated in all of the academy's top four categories.

Grammy
Awards
2020

### 2020 GRAMMYS

This was a night that Billie and Finneas will no doubt remember for the rest of their lives. They bagged a jaw-dropping five awards each. Between them, the duo won in all four main categories: Song of the Year, Album of the Year, Record of the Year, and Best New Artist. It doesn't get better than that! Finneas also won Producer of the Year for his work on Billie's album.

# MUSICAL INFLUENCES

Here are a few famous faces that have inspired Billie's musical career so far! How many of them have you heard of?

## JUSTIN BIEBER

Billie is a Belieber and has been for a LONG time. Bieber found fame in a similar way to Billie! His homemade videos were discovered on YouTube when he was just 13. Billie met Justin at Coachella festival in 2019, and this led to them releasing a remix of Billie Eilish's "bad guy."

## CHILDISH GAMBINO

As far as Billie's concerned, Childish Gambino made her. The alternative rapper has a unique R&B/hip-hop sound, with a string of hits to boot!

## AVRIL LAVIGNE

Billie has talked about how Avril's pop-punk music inspires her. Billie grew up listening to the Canadian singer! She shared on Instagram the moment she met her idol with the caption:

THANK YOU FOR MAKING ME WHAT I AM.

## LANA DEL REY

Billie admires American singer-songwriter and record producer Lana Del Rey. Lana is known for her melancholic sound, with singles including "Video Games" and "Summertime Sadness."

## TYLER, THE CREATOR

Whenever Billie talks about her musical inspiration, she mentions hip-hop star Tyler, the Creator. In case you didn't already know, he's a rapper and producer. Tyler has said that he wants to work with Billie, so stay tuned ...

## AURORA

Billie says watching the music video for Aurora's song "Runaway" was the moment she knew that making songs was what she wanted to do with her life.

"2017 Billboard Music Awards" and ELLE Present Women in Music at YouTube Space LA on May 16, 2017, in Los Angeles, California

"Pretty much my whole life I've been a performer and have loved singing and writing songs in my room for my own ears. I never thought a career as a musician was possible." —BILLIE

# THE FAN GUIDE

Want to know how to be Billie's No. 1 fan? Read these top tips to help you be the best Pirate or Eyelash EVER.

**1** Be a loud and proud member of the Pirates or Eyelashes (depending on which one you prefer!). You may just find other fans who love her as much as you do.

**2** Lend this book to a friend, or just show it to them next time you are hanging out.

**3** Support fellow members of the fandom. Billie's message is a positive one! She hates it when her fans argue or say mean things to one another. Spread the love, peeps!

**4** Be more daring and step out of your comfort zone! Billie's signature fashion style is oversized. She's not afraid to customize her clothes, either.

**5** Check out some of Billie's best music videos, if you haven't already. Turn to page 30 for our top picks.

**6** Embrace your individuality, just like she does. Don't worry about fitting in.

**7** Support causes close to your heart, just like Billie does.

**8** Look out for Billie's future tour dates. Can you imagine being able to see her performing live on stage? The dream!

# TOP BILLIE QUOTES

## ... fans

"I don't like to call them my fans because they're my family; they're the only reason I'm anything. I love my fans so much, I try to devote all my attention to them, whether it's on social media or when I see them in person."

## ... family

"I'm lucky enough to have a family that I like, and that likes me. The only reason I do what I do is because my parents didn't force me."

## ... being a role model

"I completely recognize that responsibility of being a role model. But it's not going to change the way that I am."

## ... art

"I think instead of changing the art I make, it's about letting everyone know that my art is just my way of release."

... Finneas

"I get along really well with my brother, and I always have. We're really close. We're a team."

... working in fancy studios

"No one listened to me, because I was fourteen and a girl. But we made "ocean eyes" without anyone involved—so why do I have to do this?"

"Billie's record is totally her creative vision. We make the music together, but she comes up with the album art and visual ideas, also for the live shows."

—FINNEAS

THE 62ND ANNUAL GRAMMY AWARDS, in Los Angeles, January 26, 2020

# FIND YOUR ALBUM NAME

To generate your first album name, you'll need your birth month and first initial. Look at the charts on this page and put the two words together. It's as easy as that!

## Find your birth month:

|  |  |
| --- | --- |
| January | **OCEAN** |
| February | **LIVELY** |
| March | **MYSTERIOUS** |
| April | **WONDER** |
| May | **BAD** |
| June | **PARTY** |
| July | **PIRATE** |
| August | **BORED** |
| September | **NOISE** |
| October | **INSPIRE** |
| November | **LIME** |
| December | **BOLD** |

## BE BRAVE

Grab paper and a pen to start scribbling down your song ideas. Don't worry about trying to get it right first time.

## PEACE

Find a comfy spot where you won't be disturbed. Billie likes being in her tree house—what will yours be?

## SIMPLICITY

Don't overthink it. Some of the most powerful or catchy lyrics are the simple ones!

## Find your first initial:

| | |
|---|---|
| A | LIMBO |
| B | TARANTULA |
| C | EYES |
| D | GUY |
| E | ASLEEP |
| F | FAME |
| G | EYELASHES |
| H | LOVE |
| I | SMILE |
| J | CROWN |
| K | VIVID |
| L | CREATOR |
| M | FAVOR |

| | |
|---|---|
| N | MAGICAL |
| O | FRIEND |
| P | NIGHTMARE |
| Q | ROOTS |
| R | DREAM |
| S | CLOUD |
| T | SHADOW |
| U | VISION |
| V | HONEST |
| W | GOLDEN |
| X | TRUTH |
| Y | ACE |
| Z | INTENSE |

## TRUTH

Write about something you know. Use your personal experience as inspiration and speak your truth.

## STORY LINE

Give your song a narrative with a beginning, middle, and end. Music can be an opportunity for excellent storytelling.

# MUSICAL COLORS

This gallery is a celebration of Billie's bold color choices! Check out her hair evolution.

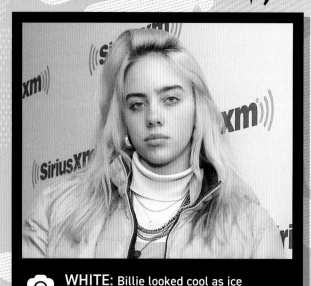

**WHITE:** Billie looked cool as ice with her white locks.

**LILAC:** Livening up her look with luscious lilac locks.

**GRAY:** Remember this smoky shade of silver?

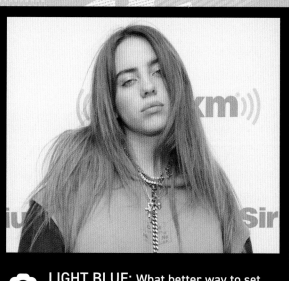

**LIGHT BLUE:** What better way to set off a blue hoodie than with blue locks?

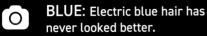

**BLUE:** Electric blue hair has never looked better.

**TURQUOISE:** We love this uber cool shade of turquoise!

**BLACK:** Making a statement with a mane of jet-black hair.

**ACID-GREEN ROOTS:** This might just be our fave look. So far . . .

# INSPIRATION AND SONGWRITING

If you're anything like us, you're in total awe of Billie's songwriting skills. It's what makes her stand out in the music industry. Read on to get a glimpse into her genius.

## SONGWRITING LESSONS

Billie and Finneas were homeschooled and encouraged to pursue their interests. Their mom taught a songwriting class so they could learn about how to structure a song. This involved listening to heaps of old music, such as Peggy Lee and Frank Sinatra! By 11 years old, Billie was making music of her own. The best thing was, Billie and her brother were allowed to stay up late as long as they were working on their music. That's some cool parents right there!

## VIVID DREAMS

Billie has talked about her experiences of sleep paralysis and lucid dreams (when the dreamer is aware of the fact that they are dreaming). She has used these dreams and night terrors as inspiration for her songs. *When We All Fall Asleep, Where Do We Go?* is all about what happens when we're in different states of unconsciousness.

## ASMR

Many of Billie's songs include elements of ASMR (autonomous sensory meridian response). Basically, ASMR involves different sounds and whispering being recorded into a microphone. Some people experience spine tingling as a result of ASMR, but it doesn't do the same thing to everyone!

## IN THE ZONE

When Billie wants to get into her writing zone, there's only one place she'll be. That's up in the tree house her dad built for her and Finneas when they were little.

"I climb up there a lot and take my ukulele and notebook in the bucket and just go up there and write."

## YOU KNOW THE DRILL

Did you know that Billie weaves recordings of everyday objects into her music? "bury a friend" features the sound of a staple gun and a dental drill, which Billie recorded from her trip to the dentist. See if you can hear them!

"When we were little, my dad would make us mix tapes with songs by artists like The Beatles and Avril Lavigne, so we learned a lot from those." —BILLIE

 KROQ Absolut Almost Acoustic Christmas 2018, Inglewood

# NO WAY!

Call yourself a superfan? Here are 9 things you would only know about Billie if you were a proper Pirate.

**1** She was named after her grandfather, Bill, who sadly passed away while her mom was pregnant with Billie.

**2** Finneas was the reason that she ended up with the middle name Pirate. He was four when Billie was born, and guess what he loved?

**3** Billie recorded background vocals for the *Diary of a Wimpy Kid* and *X-Men* movies.

**4** Billie has always been vegetarian, but she has been vegan since 2014. She cares about animal welfare and her impact on the environment.

**5** Her song "my strange addiction" includes snippets from her fave TV show, *The Office*. The track is about addictions, and this comedy series is hers.

**6** Her heritage is Irish and Scottish.

**7** A fan drew a picture of Billie crying black tears with blacked out eyes. This was then the inspiration for her "when the party's over" music video.

**8** She has opened up about living with Tourette's syndrome. The condition causes a person to make involuntary movements or sounds.

**9** Before making it big, Billie supported Florence and the Machine in 2018.

"People are terrified of me, and I want them to be."

—BILLIE

Life Is Beautiful festival, September 2019, Las Vegas

# ICONIC
## PERFORMANCES

Billie is known for her energetic live performances. Here she is in action!

📷 **92nd Annual Academy Awards, February 2020, in Hollywood, California:** Billie and Finneas performed "Yesterday" by The Beatles during the in memoriam section of the ceremony.

Glastonbury Festival, June 2019 in Glastonbury, England.

KROQ Absolut Almost Acoustic Christmas, December 2018 in Inglewood, California.

KHALID

Billie performs with Khalid at the Governors Ball Music Festival, June 2018 in New York City.

JARED LETO

Billie performs with Jared Leto at the Music Midtown Festival, September 2018 in Atlanta, Georgia.

ALICIA KEYS

Billie performs with Alicia Keys on *The Late Late Show with James Corden*, December 2019.

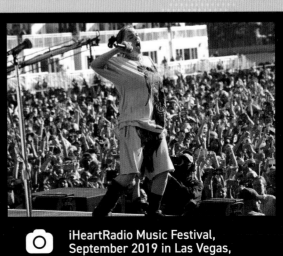

iHeartRadio Music Festival, September 2019 in Las Vegas, Nevada.

# THE FIRST WORLD TOUR

Here's the lowdown on everything you need to know about Billie's tour Where Do We Go? This epic adventure marks her first tour on a global scale!

In 2019, we saw Billie dominate the biggest festivals, and she has only gotten bigger and better in 2020 (if that was even possible!). With Billie performing hits from *When We All Fall Asleep, Where Do We Go?*, the tour started in Miami, Florida, and planned to finish in Indonesia, in Southeast Asia. Unfortunately, due to the global COVID-19 pandemic, Billie had to cancel some dates and postpone others. Her fans' safety comes before everything else!

## GLOBAL PANDEMIC

In a March 2020 tour press release, Billie told disappointed fans: "I'm so sad to do this but we need to postpone these dates to keep everyone safe. We'll let you know when they can be rescheduled. Please keep yourselves healthy. I love you."

For fans lucky enough to attend the start of the tour in Miami, Billie Eilish delivered a powerful video speech between songs, speaking out against body shaming. Check out the full speech below:

"Do you really know me?

You have opinions about my opinions, about my music, about my clothes, about my body.

Some people hate what I wear, some people praise it. Some people use it to shame others, some people use it to shame me.

But I feel you watching ... always. And nothing I do goes unseen.

So while I feel your stares, your disapproval, or your sighs of relief, if I lived by them, I'd never be able to move.

Would you like me to be smaller? Weaker? Softer? Taller?

Would you like me to be quiet?

Do my shoulders provoke you? Does my chest? Am I my stomach? My hips?

The body I was born with, is it not what you wanted?

If what I wear is comfortable, I am not a woman. If I shed the layers, I am a slut.

Though you've never seen my body, you still judge it and judge me for it. Why?

You make assumptions about people based on their size. We decide who they are. We decide what they're worth.

If I wear more, if I wear less, who decides what that makes me? What that means?

Is my value based only on your perception?

Or is your opinion of me not my responsibility?"

Text sourced from BBC News

"It's really important for kids not to think that there's something intangible and out of reach for them."

—BILLIE

 Billie performing at La Cigale on February 18, 2019, in Paris, France

# HOW WELL DO YOU KNOW BILLIE?

Take our quiz to discover your superfan status. Ready, set, GO!

**1** Name the single that Billie uploaded onto SoundCloud at age 14.

**2** How many Grammys did Billie win in 2020?

**3** What is Billie's mom's name?

**4** Do you know what her fave TV show is?

**5** Name 3 instruments that Billie can play.

**6** What does Billie call her loyal fans?

**7** Billie has a pet, but what is it?

**8** What is Billie's star sign?

**9** What Brit Award did Billie win in 2020?

**10** Who does she cowrite her music with?

**11** How many awards did Billie win at the 2019 AMAs?

**12** What is the name of her 2020 world tour?

Turn to page 80 to check your answers. Good luck!

**13** What family member was Billie named after?

**14** Who built Billie a tree house?

# WHAT NEXT FOR EILISH?

Billie's future is looking as bright as her neon clothes! From documentaries to James Bond —we can't wait to see what's next.

## SQUAD GOALS

Billie now has a devoted audience of adoring fans and fellow artists. With her ever-increasing party of Pirates, the Billie effect shows no sign of slowing down.

## INSPIRE

She's the unapologetic voice of a generation. Let's hope that she keeps inspiring young people to register to vote, speak out on the things they care about, and follow their dreams. Being young doesn't mean that your opinion doesn't count. Keep spreading the positive messages, Billie!

## GROWING

It's not just Billie's fan base that's growing—her self-confidence is, too! Thanks to the phenomenal success of her first album, plus the copious awards she's earned along the way, Billie knows people respect her as an artist. She's directed her music videos to huge praise.

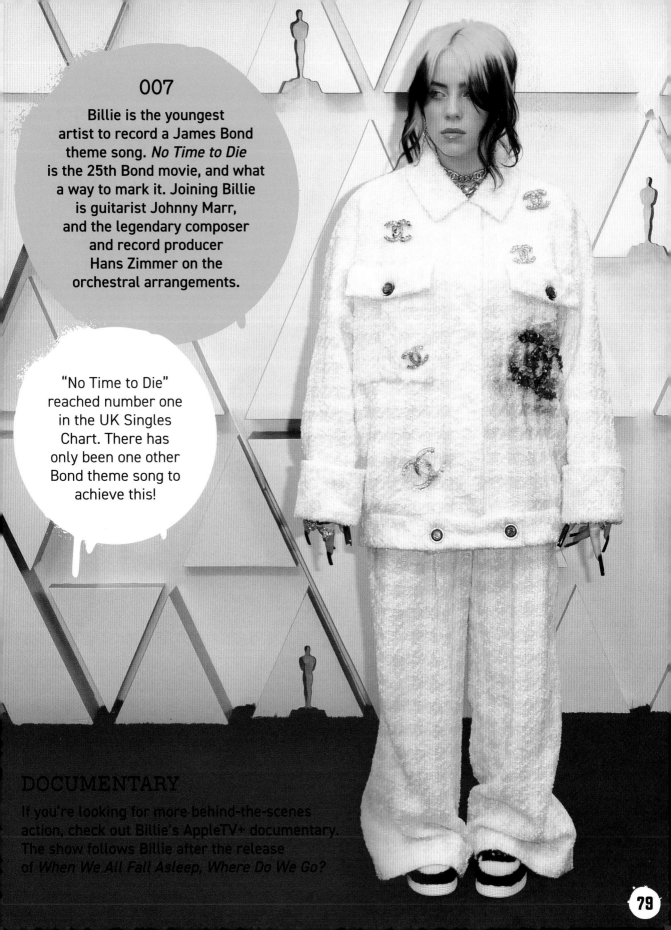

## 007

Billie is the youngest artist to record a James Bond theme song. *No Time to Die* is the 25th Bond movie, and what a way to mark it. Joining Billie is guitarist Johnny Marr, and the legendary composer and record producer Hans Zimmer on the orchestral arrangements.

"No Time to Die" reached number one in the UK Singles Chart. There has only been one other Bond theme song to achieve this!

## DOCUMENTARY

If you're looking for more behind-the-scenes action, check out Billie's AppleTV+ documentary. The show follows Billie after the release of *When We All Fall Asleep, Where Do We Go?*

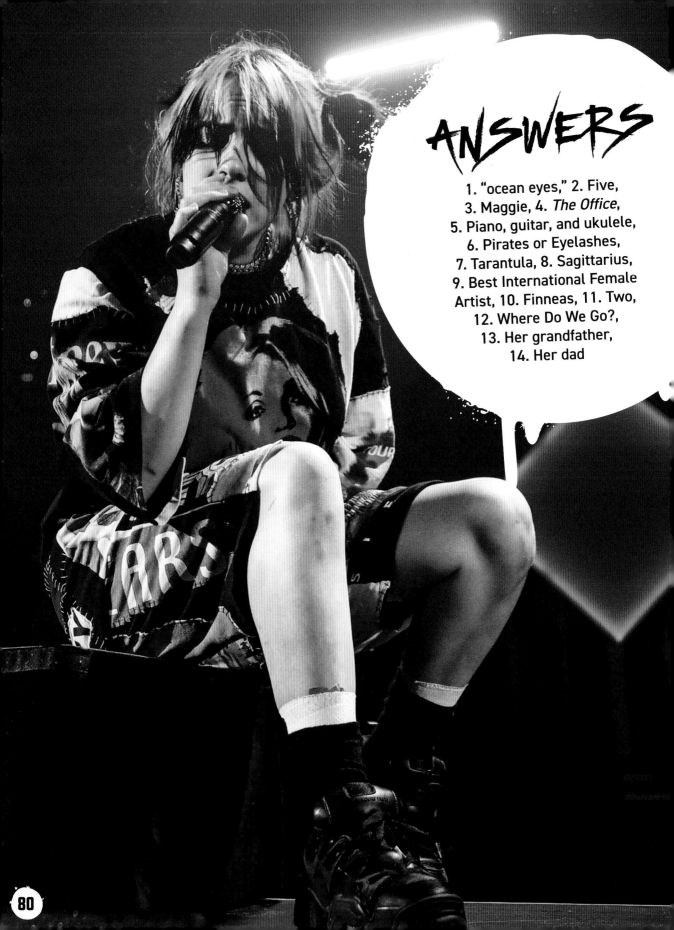

# ANSWERS

1. "ocean eyes," 2. Five,
3. Maggie, 4. *The Office*,
5. Piano, guitar, and ukulele,
6. Pirates or Eyelashes,
7. Tarantula, 8. Sagittarius,
9. Best International Female
Artist, 10. Finneas, 11. Two,
12. Where Do We Go?,
13. Her grandfather,
14. Her dad